Praise for Leah Saint Marie

"A rich, complex, sharp collection of poetry, sometimes strange and often strangely, hauntingly beautiful. Ferocious poems that are also resonant with song-like turns and tonal surprises. The double rhythms (of violence and tenderness, of animal and human, of sexual hunger and the body's losses) pull us in and hold us in thrall like a heartbeat."
– Karen Connelly, author of *The Lizard Cage* & *The Change Room*

"Diamonds. That's what the poems that inhabit Leah Saint Marie's constellational debut are: diamonds. Small and brilliant, they radiate the 'careful violence' that is so often the residue of the 'earned ache of something unfinished.' And like diamonds, the slightest turn reveals a sudden unexpected flash: some small, yet essential, detail of 'this nowness' that, without the eye of an exquisite poet, would risk being lost forever as the 'world rockets forth / in a finite trajectory.'"
– Scott Navicky, author of *Humboldt* & *If You Give Me a Lily, I'll Make It a Field : The Wexner Lectures*

"Encounters first and last, with the tides and the seasons, the cosmos, and the inner workings of the mind and the heart, in every poem a journey and a discovery."
– Meedo Taha, author of *A Road to Damascus*

"Leah Saint Marie's voice is just as savage as it is vulnerable. Her ability to balance all the intricate complexities of family dynamics on a line of well-crafted prose left me aching."
 – Morgan Nikola-Wren, author of *Magic with Skin On*

"Leah Saint Marie's kaleidoscopic collection of poetry...evokes a young Patti Smith quality in identifying the prosaic or quotidian moments in life and relates them to the Natural World and, in some cases, the incomprehensible emptiness of eternity. [S]he taps into the irry relationship between the raw essence of Nature and our own wants and insatiable needs we identify and chase after in life. By observing the Earth and its creatures, she brings out a more profound truth about our own place in the sometimes unforgiving reality of existence. She is unapologetic in her exploration of the dirty true emotions that can overwhelm and recalibrate our lives. She closes the collection with an unfiltered set of poems about coming of age, first experiences, and the marks they leave on the soul. Her final poem, 'Five Blackbirds,' is a luminous finish to this lush and far-reaching tapestry of poetry."
 – Theo Salter, Writer for the Owl & Pussycat Theatre Co.

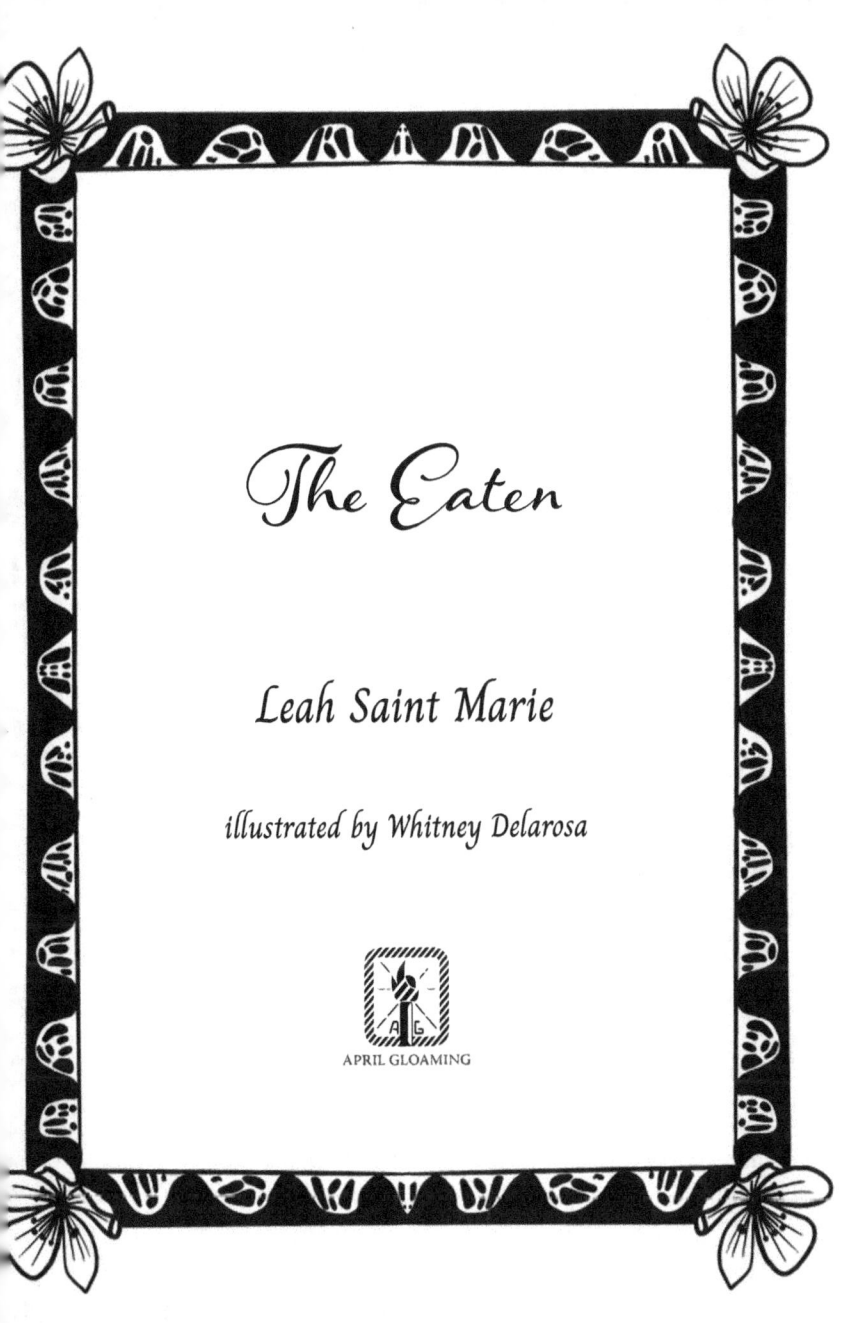

The Eaten

Leah Saint Marie

illustrated by Whitney Delarosa

APRIL GLOAMING

Publisher's Cataloguing-in-Publication Data

Saint Marie, Leah
    The eaten / written by Leah Saint Marie
    ISBN: 978-1-953932-20-4

1. Poetry: General 2. Poetry: American - General 3. Poetry: Women Authors I. Title II. Author

Library of Congress Control Number: 2023945826

For Sarah,
who stayed with me through all of the moments herein.

Contents

Let's Start at the End.

New Kingdom	13
Field Dressing	14
Winter	15
The Photographer: Italy, 1918	16
Evelyn	17
Eril Andrade	18
Mighty Mighty	19
Nine Minutes	20
The Waltz	21

Father

Farmboy	25
Work	26
The Hunter	28

Contents

Creation

All the Pretty	33
The Architect	35
Dirty Glass	36
Ursa Minor	37
Old Kingdom	38
On the Pier	39
Fear	41
Plan B	43
Waking	44
Blackbird in the Morning	45
Valentine's Day Poem	46
First Act	47
The Elk	48
Blackbird	49
First Draft: For Anton	50
The Garden	51

Violence

Cult of Winter	55
Seed	56
All Hail the Living	58
Systems	59
Thief	60
Your Kingdom	61
Lessons	62

Contents

Mother's Journal Entries

18 Aug 197-	67
30 May 198-	68
4 December 198-	69
29 September 199-	70
16 January 200-	71
1 May 201-	72
30 October 197-	73

Sex

Summer 1991	77
First Orgasm	79
Clit	80
Marcello	81
Sestina in Blonde	82
The Snow	84
New Year's Eve	85
Turn Me Up	87
Old Lovers	88
Tuesday	89
Poseidon	91
Anus	92
Trinitia Church	93
Snakebite	94
Splintered	95
Morning	96

Contents

Contrition	97
Bloodsong	98
Block Island	99
The Thirst	100
Father	101
In Dreams	102
Yellow Suit	103
The Searcher	104
Spatial Recognition	105
The Man Who Sleeps	107
Farewell Ceremony	108
After the Rape	110
Red Light	111
The Cage	113
Mornings	114
Black Holes	115
Salt	116
Galaxies	117
Five Blackbirds	118

Let's Start at the End.

New Kingdom

Everywhere there is accusing space
between me and you, and you and God,
and all other entities
including the fox
who is castled by his urges;
and this is like being a man
living with the bullet's possibility.

Death stalks in the field,
pinions your life to corn silk
and turns your blue heart
into a wind-up toy,
apathetic to its chirps
from rising brambles.

Death digs a space inside,
burrows in the dark intimacy
of your fear,
sharp as the word
thistle.

Field Dressing

I am nine years old sitting near the porch
where I hear the song of blood
pool into a tin pail.

My grandfather sticks his fingers into the deer
and rents fur from meat.
Heat hits his face.

He is seventeen years dead
so it is in dreams I hunt with him.
I bury my body into the earth;
there is no sound and the smell of ozone
cracks above the frozen field.
The rifle calls in short bursts
a flute with one note.

I have found it—
I have lost the word
but I have found it.

Winter

You just lay your kids to bed.
There are snowflakes falling
past the front porch light
and I feel the urge to fit
my mouth to you and taste milk
muscled past your lips
so when I kiss you
you taste chilled and sour.

Outside nothing speaks.
There are six steps
to the front door
I don't take.

An owl breaks bones in a nearby tree;
shapes its feet into fists, quarters
the dead field mouse
then takes flight into the dark theatre.

The Photographer: Italy, 1918

During the end of The First World War,
returning soldiers were embraced by loved ones,
and thus, the second and third wave
of Spanish Influenza spread.

The war ends: women embrace soldiers
who are as awkward to hold as sand.
The veteran photographer snaps a photo in Sorrento
as a woman slips behind his camera,
grazie, turns his face to her—

She takes him home with her
where a grove of lemon trees eats
the side of a mountain
with its crooked jaw line.

The sun is setting. The woman snaps a lemon
off a branch, dimpled and shiny. She splits
it with her mouth—its sharpness fills
the air between them. She tosses it up laughing,
pulp curled round her tongue. The photographer's ready,
takes the shot, coughs—it's beginning.

A bat snatches the fruit from its arc.
He circles twice above them hungry;
he's never been so hungry.

Evelyn

Evelyn, Evelyn won't you come out and play
with your smoky moods and crooked smile?

She fishes her hand in her mouth past the gullet hoping.
Drags her hand past the paste-like viscera.
Where is it? Where can that backbone be.

All she finds
a caged bird coughing—
covered in parasites,
everything feeding.

Eril Andrade

A found poem taken from Ian Urbina's article in The New York Times, *"Tricked and Indebted on Land, Abused or Abandoned at Sea"*

His family receives him in a pine coffin—
jet black from the fish freezer.
He's missing an eye and his pancreas.
An autopsy reveals the Filipino man
had been inflicted with cuts and bruises.

His mother's roof leaks
on a note taped to his body
hand-written in Chinese.

The local prosecutor interviews
the family in February. They said they waited—
their silence a gatekeeper.

In Singapore, there are a dozen other men missing,
they eye Eril's family with suspicious destiny
waiting for the knock at the door—the rooty smell of pine.

Mighty Mighty

Oh mighty heart!
With your four windows boarded up
for the hurricane of loss you've been promised
by every movie,
magazine,
parent.

Do you think you grow by not breaking?
Do you think fear is a better guest
than the hungry wolves in their dinner jackets
outside your door?

Nine Minutes

The butterfly's tongue—
sharp and golden—
roots for the sweetest flower;
knows her name by taste.

If I kiss you after our time empties
like a long river into the brackish delta
I do not think I'll know you.
So whose name should I call
when you answer your phone tomorrow
when I cannot use it now to keep you?

The Waltz

One day you will die and I'll remember you however it is I wish to and then I'll follow you there, to wherever. Then who will know you and the way you argued with your hip cocked out and your face half in the bedroom doorframe blaming me? Or how you spoke gruff as a winter bear in the morning because a dream was still caught in the back of your throat? Or how you licked the last bit of syrup from my fork with a fox-licking-the-chicken-blood grin, stuck now in this book's crevice heated by the palms of hot-blooded lovers who swear that when God so made them he invented love?

And who now will be left to blame this poet of such foolish love stories when the whole world's ending, and you and I are nowhere left to see it burn, but dancing in the wherever?

Father

Farmboy

He's twelve or almost.
He wears his father's gun and looks
as locusts wire all other sounds shut
and the boy with a scar on his chin sings
so quiet no god can hear him.

There are things not yet missing in him
so there is a careful way he slides the coyote
from his shoulders and the scar adjusts to white
as the boy shouts at birds and dances.

The coyote looks rusted on the weeds—
a dull copper color matted with burrs and urine.
The boy hooks the eye and exhumes it—

takes out the marbled lens
so he can look through it
and see death perpetually coming
in variegated and borrowed skin.

Work

Outside, bright pine and sun;
the tree bough twists up—
my father breaks paper wasps with his hands—
a parade of dead curve to the earth.
He steals the bones of their voice
outside my window.

My father has a tattoo of a window
on his arm. He scratches at it, *To let in the sun*
he says in his father's voice—
as if his drawl rises up
from the cussed earth—
he claps his hands,

he sings, claps his hands,
sings; his mouth a broken window
and I look inside. Above wet earth
I see the late sun
rage at his back and it goes up
the mountains like a voice.

My father's fist repeats like a voice—
he buries his hands,
that look like his father's hands, up
to his wrists until he cannot feel the fear outside his window.
I hear him singing, *I am not done,* to the sun
I am not yet, to the earth.

I have seen him bury his words in earth,
I am of this, his voice
steals me like a piece of luck gone bad; sun
on his hands
that breaks its ribbons through my window;
lying on the floor I hear him, all the way up

in my room. When he comes home late, close up
he smells of rank earth.
He takes a spot by the window
and stares down the day and rations his voice
until there is enough he doesn't say. I look at his hands.
From inside our house, I know there is no sun.

My father claps the sun in his hands and breaks his voice
in the wasp's ear. He says to the blue creature, *This is my window,*
　　take it.

The Hunter

Oh hunter, where are you going—
doubling your gunny sack?

Lo the headwinds push you back
as you pray to 13 gods
for a new buckskin.

All the amber-yellow eyes dart
your arrow tip
as you sink further
into piney wood.

Now the jackrabbit
and the tiny sparrow shadows
your assassination
and death pastes the broken stems.

Sticky with blood and thistle
you build an animal totem
bound with leather and fresh bone
topped off with the first lover's head—
your starry sorrow shining—
the thing you cannot kill.

Creation

All the Pretty

I am many selves;
the wingtip and the throated
ee-oh-lay, ee-oh-lay.

Through the juvenile leaves
the under-muted alarm probes.

Fragmented flute-clear song
gravity pulls the spotted-white breast.

I laud the wing decline
from limb to fingertip
and bear the thrush's nickel eye.

A thousand piney insects
and their death rattle.

I forage through lowlands.
All I am—a white eye-ring,
the thrush's camouflage
the nest and the parasite
and the bold rain.

Denseness flanks below the canopy—
I long for something else.

I have sifted through abundance
foraging between sex and time.

Mixed echoes—
machine-gun like
in the understory.

Make the recluse a thrush—
give me large trees.

I am scaled down
and the thrush speaks uncaged.

The triangle in my throat pulses.
If you speak now
say the word home.

Leah Saint Marie

The Architect

Oh the impermanence of the cosmic spine
that collapses and leaves me wanting.
I cast shadows in my bloodline.

Calliope calls and I cannot divine
her answers from my haunting—
Oh the impermanence of the cosmic spine.

Here hallowed, here holed in the pine.
Were I dead, yet hear the chorus chanting.
I cast shadows in my bloodline.

I lay the heart rot, I play my life supine.
My dreams are rudderless and daunting.
Oh the impermanence of the cosmic spine.

I cannot retaliate against the immeasurable incline
of the unsung selves ever-taunting.
I cast shadows in my bloodline.

I am violated into storied line—
where I know the complexity of distance mounting.
Oh the impermanence of the cosmic spine.
I cast shadows in my bloodline.

Dirty Glass

None of it is true; not the east river falling over itself at midnight begging for me to touch it or the more distant shores of Coney Island laid up in hibernation for the winter, trashed and yearning to break into some nostalgic brilliance. The D train I take from your apartment is late and the echoes of angels down the black gulping mouth of the subway tunnel ignore me as they learn a new song. There's is an electric hum and suddenly all of you flits into me: the naked pulse of your voice ached into a question, your hands wrapped in my hair as you braid it, your bare feet slouching to the bathroom so soft as to not wake me up. As if you studied bears in the woods near suburbs to know best how to sneak right up to the dining room window and look in longing to have hands. To eat with such dexterity. To pluck the final berry from the stem and drop it in its bursting-juice entirety into your mouth. And as the train finally comes I love you like this—the image of you in your PJ bottoms the soles of your feet smudged, your bladder full as you tiptoe from me and my mouth tastes like blackberries, last of the season, hidden from wasps in the thorn thicket of their home and yes, the angels know their song by now, and your question keeps me up until it's time to go, and the inky river will keep begging and I'll forget again to do the dishes before I go but you'll forgive me as you cup your mouth to the dirty glass and say my name.

Leah Saint Marie

Ursa Minor

All day for four days I thought it was raining,
and the lie has kept me company—
an excuse to stay in as the world rockets forth
in a finite trajectory.

My aim ten years ago was an arrow
that sparked in my hand.

All arrows want to know the inside of a bear's skull—
the constellation of thought unraveled,
displaced from its dictionary of stars.

If I let go the string, dare I watch for failure or for death?
A fifth day of rain or stars?

Old Kingdom

When you were a boy you slept
with your cat's soft ear to your chin,
his purr a rocket in you—
and your mother called your hands *untamed*
and *wildings* because you never fit them
in your pockets
just so.

Now, life scratches at your ribcage
and takes your treasures out like old medals
locked in an ammo case
ruined and browned from flooding
so that your children can't tell what it was
you were proud of with those
once-upon-a-time gold stars.

You pour a tall glass of milk
and drink barefoot in your dark kitchen
and stand far from your old desire to reach
your hand out very
very slowly toward a lion
and touch him, behind his ear—
soft as dandelion seed.

Leah Saint Marie

On the Pier

She wears a swimsuit in the French style,
puckers her mouth at a joke she doesn't know
then flicks her wet hair into a loose braid.

The trumpet player on the boardwalk lips
his horn and blows
and suddenly the ocean knows regret
that it has no mouth.

As the music comes
the girl spots an old boat anchored
past the breakers.
Inside she imagines
the captain eats cold soup from a can—
cannot compare his life to any other.

The captain pauses between bites—
the trumpet's notes come soft—
a sudden flash and it's 1965—
he's in his father's blue Mustang—
a girl he likes slinks her hand around his neck
runs her fingers up and down—
plays his scales;
the flicker ghost of love.

The song ends.
The captain's alone.
The trumpeter packs it in.
The girl on the beach is now cold—
wraps her thin arms around herself—
a flower when the sun goes down,
an inky bee just born.

Fear

(Tranströmer found poem)

One-by-one the long-observed saints
suckle the fallen bird—
laugh at beauty.

Here, swallow this spirit
taste the ebb and break of life.
Help me keep something alive.

I live in transparency—
a portrait of a mirror,
a god of measurements;
survival vs. winter,
the animal vs. stillness.

I find many enemies in the evening
queuing at my door.
They're vigilant—undivided shadows.
Parts of us are living
or murmuring.

If I close my eyes for ten minutes
the expression is the same.
The many one-ness of the frozen crowd knocking—
to live under a smearing of eyes,
not many but one.

In my hands I hold the clay,
not grains of sand.

Plan B

The wolf sounds her lament somewhere in the far-off wood.
She wants to sing her sadness for me as I read the instructions on
my bottle.

There is a sound an infant makes fat from mother's milk—
its entire body sated.

And now you think one begets the other: the animal and the babe;
loneliness and need. I tell you there is no difference. Each erases
the outline of their autonomy.

I close my mouth and swallow one pill then walk outside and find
all things in the distance are clear as the darkness behind the sun.

The wolf pads farther off, folds her voice on snow. The infant
sleeps somewhere in me unrealized.

Waking

Last night I displaced constellations.
I was snow in someone else's dream.
I knew brightness waking; watch me, I am elations.

In borrowed skin I shouted exaltations
until black eclipsed my conscious stream.
Last night I displaced constellations.

All my rivered thoughts and ruminations
lay their dying embers in this body's dream.
I knew brightness waking; watch me, I am elations.

My bright body knew all abstract meditations
existing between nothingness and supreme.
Last night I displaced constellations

until my marrow shook like some dying star's reverberations.
I unshouldered limits of a waking life's regime.
I knew brightness waking; watch me, I am elations.

I shouted infinitesimal heavens until all destinations
beckoned me hither with euphoric scream.
Last night I displaced constellations.
I knew brightness waking; watch me, I am elations.

Leah Saint Marie

Blackbird in the Morning

Strange that after an eon of evolution
we still don't know each other
enough to say hello—this blackbird and I.

His body a small compass of need roots
through the wood's cellar
where his voice pitches
ee-oh-lay ee-oh-lay
between bites of spider.

By mid-morning a million cells are reinvented
in his twig legs and in mine
the earned ache of something unfinished—
the awful biology of my shortcomings.

Like this the blackbird sings to me.
I want to tell him I haven't even learned Italian yet.

But sometimes a small vessel breaks
into my wilderness
and blows the dust off.

Valentine's Day Poem

Kill the "I,"
put it on a plate—
with the knife's edge, eat it.
Have all of it.
Even the devil tail of its ghost.

Then do what everyone does
after a suicide.
Be beautiful for a day.

And do what you want
with your beauty
and your day—

eat the liquid sun,
break your sex,
drink this poem.

The three buttons to love wait
with such terrible promise.

First Act

I want to button the loosed button on your shirt so badly I forget
to breathe and so fumble over the words *May I,* as I flit my fingers
by your throat where I know something as abstract as grace waits;
something they misname by calling it manly, stoic, simple.

I know your courage is conquered when a beautiful woman calls
your name in the dark of your room, reaches for you naked, and
feels her way to you. Your voice unprisoned says, *Closer, I'm here.*

The Elk

Imagine the empty world.
And inside this newness an arrow;
small, gold at the edges, a stab
of light in the immovable now.

And this arrow is something once dormant
locked in a box in the basement,
or beneath the bed—
something only the spiders speak to.

Life has condensed into singularities:
the epiphany at the traffic light;
the ribboned song of a long-waited text;
the perfect bite of toast.

There was and will always be nothing
and everything;
this aria of words to placate death,
and the sentence of fog
where elk dance pollen
off their hooves.

Blackbird

My flushing call bursts
atop limbs.
Oh watch this blackbird dance—
know my careful violence.

I sound in the brilliant forests.
I hunt through all shades of green—
the wreck of throttled emptiness—
the salt-ring ache of winter.

Here the trumpet sounds—
hear it quake in the bottomless
midnight of sky.

Lo do I see my kin tumble
like stars.
They dance like the sharpest urge.
Oh let it go;
let me sing my skin to dust
or let me own this sight forever.

First Draft: For Anton

I have seen infinity—even while my grief mothers me do I see it.

It shows me all the things I am afraid to touch—the man retrieving the letter from the mailbox, he walks like he's already forgiven me and the dialogue of his love is a 35mm image locked in a gesture of giving.

Not even the cutting room floor can translate this moment well enough to predict what is to come. Tarkovsky and de Sica grip their wrists to know this failure.

Sometimes there are lifelike diamonds too bright to look at, cut like a cubist painting, burning.

Leah Saint Marie

The Garden

You bite the tiger tomato—
juice thick with seeds
a sticky syrup
reflects you.

I count each seed—
seven worlds owned by you.

What will you make them?
Soil or food?

You, god of this sex between us.
What makes you smile at me
when we know all there is to know of each other?

In your other hand a second tomato.
I lean in and see the feathered edge of your eyelashes
pregnant with juice.

The blue whip flame of your eyes. My heart
the size of the thing you bite
and you bite.

Violence

Cult of Winter

Pain is the small marbled heart
of a rabbit beating
in the first imprint of snow.

Here I find the universal truth
that even the selfish sun
despairs a kinship.

I see the tracks in snow, the rush—
wild dissonance—
unplanned, followed by the fox.

I do not know whom I root for—
predator or prey—
but what else is life
except measures of violence
untamed beneath the thorn bush?

My heart joined by many others running—
the fox and rabbit; we,
the unfortunate lords.

Seed

I scooped out a pile of your ash
and put it in a mason jar.
Placed it on the bedroom dresser
so that when I dreamt of you
I could wake up and yell at you.

Trapped and dirty in that jar
you said nothing.

And I didn't care
that you were not a ghost
like you promised.

I put your picture in the ground
in my backyard
where we once kissed
and listened to the slow fruit drop
from the tree.
I pushed a seed into the ground
above your smile,
wanting you to taste
the things to come.

Leah Saint Marie

And every day for two seasons
I'd go to that seed
in the stubborn ground
and care for it
so that one day
the roots would come
to tangle,
choke,
and pull you apart.

All Hail the Living

I am even afraid of this blank page—
cut of the guillotine's blade,
it goes through the quick of me
and all I held as sacred—
the idea of myself as a great artist, hero, mother
becomes something else to be buried.
I would keep it so—
this fear like an egg in my belly,
seed of my future crimes.

Last night I dreamt my first lover
set himself on fire—I was jealous of this too.

All my life I wanted to be fire,
to burn everything as I danced with
men in my belly.

Even when I died,
they would check on me,
unsure.

Systems

The child cries, but it's useless.
She holds out her hand waiting.
Her mother hums
each note, trips on the stairs as she goes.
The first lesson is always betrayal.

Tomorrow her teacher will ask what she dreamt,
but it's nothing, a long void, irreverent, slick.

She'll chew her bottom lip as she says—
her mouth sour with breakfast milk—
the dreams don't come.
I close my eyes and it's this.

She'll hold her hands together,
an invisible planet.

Her mother's hand pulls away,
the close of her bedroom door,
something infinite lost.

Thief

I spit the seeds out,
their promise stolen.
Each hard pellet
I break
open its mouth
and see a reversed flower,
who will never kiss
the Spanish dancers.

Even now
the future botanist grows
his hate for me,
as his wife mourns
in the next room
where only the sun
dares touch her.

Your Kingdom

My corpulent bodied gods yell
at your corpulent bodied gods
as your violence twists around ennui
while you wear that look at the breakfast table
these past nine years.

You once asked me what names the Vikings cried
when they thirsted on the battlefield. I said not yours,
and you laughed with their howl in your voice.

You stare out your bedroom window
and by the slice of your stillness
I can tell no one cut the heavy head
of a rose from another's garden
and passed its redolent body
closer to your lips than any other body,
and it is this need
that keeps you staring into other people's lives
with a detest and longing of a king
too long looking at the severed head of his wife.

Lessons

You hum the song your mother taught you
three decades ago. I take this in too—
this pilgrimage from your past—
the borrowed timbre
of her voice from you fills
the space to come.

If you should lift your hand to seal
the door to my bedroom, then waste
its skill to hail a cab,
I shall forever hate the sound
of a man humming, and think
his voice a harbinger
of destruction, a substitute
for the bugle at dawn.

Oh requiem for carnage,
what has your mother taught you?

Mother's Journal Entries

Leah Saint Marie

18 Aug 197-

I turn the things I love to myths.

I. My mother's aria that she taught me when she was younger and prettier than me.

I begin the letter to my husband: *The only reason birds sing is because they hate silence. So when I open our bedroom window in the morning, violence hums in trees.*

I take the letter and wrap it into an origami boat.

Journal entry: *If he said anything, it would sound like a sad man dancing in an old suit.*

II. When the hummingbird lifts its head from my daughter's touch, the two wrapped in so much spun gold I could not tell them apart. Yes, then you will know what I know, then you will ache how I ache.

30 May 198-

Grief disguises itself,
circles the old hill twice
and settles as an old dog settles.

4 December 198-

I am wasp-eaten
the curdled milk core of me
edged past desire.

29 September 199-

Nightmares.

Each one shifts its face
from one muddied color to the next.

I hear the slick pump of their hearts
as they practice their awkward walk toward me.

16 January 200-

God's an animal
covered in dirt and urine
now digging at me.

1 May 201-

Two cocoons open
split, twisted, the small secret
of their birth obscene.

Leah Saint Marie

30 October 197-

A woman who liked the smell of gun smoke waited on her porch holding the desert of her hands together.

A man who lived his entire life just to be left alone sits in the running car in the spring of 19— before they invented the possibility of the moon.

and so it hangs unsullied above them and cuts cold lengths of shadows across tilled earth where perennials will brave their heads beside the red, two-story house, and it is a house just long enough to be sold by their eldest son who as yet still dreams young-boy dreams upstairs of dumb animals felled by his new buck knife.

And this is when a crow should cry in the not-yet-rotted tree and mourn a private loss loudly. The woman takes her rifle, aims an expert shot, then for the second time that night, steel recoils into her soft shoulder.

The boy will wake in the morning, see his father's car gone and his mother an unbent triangle in bed. And he'll go outside, lift the crow by its wings then pluck the feathers for a makeshift crown he'll wear—king of his new castle. He'll wait for the queen to wake and admire the blue-black bruise of feathers across his head.

Sex

Leah Saint Marie

Summer 1991

It's the first summer I have breasts.
I admire where they curve—
a slip of shadow
the accident where the artist's brush lingered too long.

My swimsuit is too tight—
the wet bone in the lion's mouth.

The boy in the pool
a champagne flute
that dives under.

I open my legs and let him see
the architecture of my sex
where the jungle beasts gather
to sharpen their hunger.

The slap of water.
The sharp breath of chlorine.
I shut my eyes to see it—
to know him looking at me.

I am delirious—
transfixed by my pubic bone
hard as a horn.

Where the mothers sunbathe
a crown of that bone
points up at their god.

When I step from the pool
there's the rush of water down my leg
a snake out of its skin.

First Orgasm

I remember the shock and chill—
a close whisper that knocked
all the closed doors of my body—
stuck in the very middle of youth—
open.

It's brief—
something between the seen and the unseen—
this water passing through me.
The marrow song in me,
digging.

I am nothing but this water—
this serpent eye—
this nowness.

My finger a kite string—
the atom thread that proves
the radical impossibility
of the ocean—
divided by eons
and the many mouths
of animals—
finding itself again
in this,
the clear glass
of my body.

Clit

You, more so than all
know the interior map
of men's mouths begging

you open as they
open—star of my body
teach them how to sing.

Marcello

His photograph—everything after the snap
and flash indelible—the ink
of heartbreak.

To rewind the film
an hour before his smile
and lift of chin
that caught the lens
and flared with sudden life.

Then the frames between
where I imagine he lingers—
the space when he closed my door
and pressed his ear to it, shut his eyes,
held his breath and thought,
Listen, she's humming—
the sound of a butterfly taking off—
as my slip hits the floor.

Sestina in Blonde

I touched her toes—pink glossy—in my throat a large animal.
I swallowed to keep from kissing her. Oh summer!
The heat of you. I wanted to shave my head.
To pierce my skin with hot needles.
I was almost twelve and knew the storm of years
I'd yet to live in order to claim that kiss.

Then there was Anne and she wouldn't kiss
but held my hand as we walked the quad, my animal
to her grace. Her violet skirt snapping. Years
later I still hear it. Song of my summer.
Her tattooed hip a petal. I trace the outline of needles
as we drift to sleep, two question marks head to head.

New Year's Eve in black mascara, I turn a pretty girl's head.
She follows me, slick shaved I touch her, then we kiss.
I pull her lace thong down. Her fingers—needles
through my hair. She's sixteen—an animal
used to heady scents. I'm close but pull my summer
from her knowing. I'll regret it for years.

Leah Saint Marie

I push through the violent storm of my twenties, the years
as white snow, frozen in the black box of my head.
But then there's Pittsburgh and Erin and that summer
we moved in together. Her expensive rose perfume a kiss
I inhale from her pillow. It turns my animal
inside out. How to say it—love buzzes like needles.

Then there is no one. I paint a different color, I use needles
to mark my arm black. If I tell you I have nothing but years,
will you tell me a parable where the animal
walks away from the wall so when everything falls in my head
this feeling ends? I don't miss it. I'm lying. Will you give me a kiss?
Will you plant it just so on the back of my knee in high summer?

Men ask me—brown wolf mouths gaping—about my summer.
They want and they want and they want. And I feel needles
from their want of me; their sex is not a kiss.
If I am a dictionary, no, if I am the Torah, no if I am years
and ephemeral, then I am only a head.
The emotion of me the only truth—not even an animal.

Absent of needles in my many heads, I'm both human and animal.
I want the kiss at the end of years, of the first summer.

The Snow

I dreamt of snow
stretched like a white fox humming.
I knew this was all the broken men whose
anger I ate kiss by kiss,
whom I fucked until their sorrow tore at the bedroom door—
like a shadow with no legs—
so loudly the old dog downstairs
grew his hate for me.

These broken men and I know
what the swimmer knows
diving into opaque water—
the tacit contract—
that coming here means you agree
to no longer own yourself.

I fill my hands with snow
until they go blue.
I drink so that when my next lover
cups his ear to my belly—
holds his breath—
he'll hear the fox humming.

New Year's Eve

At the party I cannot swallow
as he leads me to his bedroom.
Past the windows I see
trees in coats too small
their white wrists stick out.

Then, all sound is sucked
from the room so only his eyes
have voice—this beggar,
his cock like a fulcrum
by which we descend
into the hell where lovers lie.

I take him in my mouth
and know how stars are born.

In the alter of this moment he stares,
jealous of the details in the mirror—
my stocking in his fist
rings his fingers like a tongue of branches through the snow.

He leaves my mouth like a sigh.
He is barely breathing
as still as David's statue in Borghese
locked in the artist's hands.

85

The Eaten

It's New Year's Eve.
We hesitate to feed
the distance between us
as the world begins its countdown.

Leah Saint Marie

Turn Me Up

The man beside me at the bar leans over three empty beer bottles,
grabs my hand and slurs something untranslatable.

We're both here for the jazz man on stage
who plays the piano
like a first kiss caught on film—
irrevocable.

How to explain to you
that jazz turns me inside out—
and outside the body's fortress
an army of nerves
rages.

Reversed like this my damned heart captains me—
hardly a word is needed.

The jazz man knows this and urgent he sings the body,
holds my army inside his notes.

How else is jazz except like this,
translated through the anarchy of love.

Old Lovers

They do not shake me like a bad dog that likes the beating.

I misstep desire for a piece of paper with my name on it left on the dresser with the musk of hope.

Get the camera ready. Tie me in knots with delicate practice. Countersink the headboard with the farmer's tools.

The Russian in New York lives next to my sadist voyeur. Don't make me choose between ill- equipped and selfish when there's Manuel Ferrara who can love my pussy better in a French whisper than a 28-year-old with large hands.

If I could repeat the last ten years, I'd have fucked that Thai man with the pretty smile who could not swim.

In Phuket I watched a monk kick a collarless dog to death for his past-life crimes. Admire my naked neck, tie the bootstraps tight. Don't mistake love for what this is.

Tuesday

All day there's been this sigh
caught in my body
as I move about
from bed to shower
from breakfast to lunch
from the blank spaces
of this Tuesday.

If I give it a word
it is fuck
with the vowel stretched
as an alligator neck
you risk your own to see the end of.

It is a sigh you put in me
as I flash through Sunday morning
and what we did
and what you said
and the silhouette of you
in my bathroom door
as I showered,
watching.

Now, I lie in bed
on unwashed sheets
that hold the wilding kingdom
of you breaking
and breaking
and breaking
me open.

Poseidon

O earthquake god
I open you
look inside—
your shark-black heart ticks
a slick metronome
as I wait here
in this windowless cave.

Don't pretend to me exile is a gift
you give to me each year.

I know your trick—your tethered heart
a noose around me.

And I, I fear stillness darling.
And you are like a shark that waits for me,
its jaws clicking like many clocks.

I wonder at you,
what it is that you cherish so
when you can't even know me
beyond sacrifice.

I smell your salt body
before you enter the room.
I see the cut of fin—
sharpest blade.

Anus

Pearl of my body
hidden all day from man's sight
softest part of me.

Trinitia Church

Your eyes, two black birds following
every angle of the ceiling, the stoic stained saints,
my face upturned to you. Bucolic frescoes breeding
with angelic friezes. Gaeta,
translating itself, points one finger to the sky.

The basilica drowns in the shadow of Monte Orlando.
The Turk's Grotto eats three crevices in the mountain.
Your fingers hush me.
A handprint as acquiescence to faith.

Prayer like the sound of a shirt falling.

Christ's body hangs; his power to suffer
and seduce. The words *Venus Significant Humanitatem:*
Love is not the sum of us.

Chianti circles your lips; Bacchus grin, you run
your finger over it and wet my mouth.

Snakebite

I pick dry scales off tile—
echo of my diamond back.
There must be love here
even as the venom
sits in my kiss
writing its own poem.

Splintered

Every spider for some reason
loves my face.
While I'm sleeping,
when I go hiking,
whenever I stick my head up a tree,
there she is, waiting.

It's as if her
kaleidoscope of knowledge
of my nose,
awkward in the middle
of my sudden face
has equally shocked her.

We have a tacit agreement:
I don't kill her
and she doesn't kill me
and we live so separate
and invisible from each other
that the heartbreak of our lives
is a secret in all the quiet places.

Morning

So sudden was my body
unribboned from sleep
that I do not know myself.

Shifted from thought to animal
I am all hunger and sex—
both skin and first instinct.

I hear the beast's din
in my arteries,
and the thin want of my body.

My bedroom sounded like copper falling.
At first bite you spill treasures—
a vein of bright-rubied loss.

I am predation and fuck—
a whistle-thin vision
of animal at dawn—
all my fur golden.

Contrition

I dress myself in my mother's mood.
I try it on and feel as the spring snake feels
stretching in its new scales.

I pull her over my eyes and see these strangers—
call them father, call them brother.
I try to touch them, but they shirk
as an owl who's dazed
from the effort of the sun.

I wait for my mother's voice
as my own, telling me the snake
is a sly thing,
changing its skin every few seasons.

I see her face when I look in the mirror.
I will tell this mirror everything.

Bloodsong

The small bloodsong of my life
crawled out from a shadow
and I knew with the certainty of a god
if I unzipped my skin
and reached inside
there would be mountains of fleeced gold.

Block Island Trip

You have our mother's face
and hide it when water breaks
against you, and you flinch.
It's the horizon that sees you then
instead of my camera.
You keep the secret
of what you look like
when no one's watching.

You walk out into the water
and go very far
until I can no longer see
the bladed curve of your back.

There is a line stretching
from me to you and you
to something in the past
you have not named.
With great effort you lean
into September and the ocean
is so loud
that when I call
you cannot hear your own name.

The Thirst

I drink this glass of water
barefoot in the kitchen
after all the assassinations of the day
have left me,

and I am only this adultery of silence,
that takes me piece by piece.

How welcome to stand so naked—

the snake with fresh skin,
the pause before waking.

I tilt my head back until the glass is empty—
and yet this thirst,
all my life
burdened by it.

Leah Saint Marie

Father

He doesn't speak, so I don't speak,
and every hour of daylight is a muted chorus.

How curious a world sucked of sound
so that only the doing exists.

Only the frail moments of living
when the compact and tired man
sits down to watch tv.

There is no aria of spring compares to him.

He stuffs his hands in his pockets.
All his days of fellowship past,
his life this onceness.

And yet, there are things
he still needs to tell me.
Yes, there are things—
many, many things.

In Dreams

I'm a tree branch breaking in slow motion. Winter thickens over me heavy as a kiss unanswered. Sometimes I dare myself to break and fall. And sometimes years pass and I hang there like my father's loneliness, his fast-hearted love like moth wings beating from the light—he looks like a thread of silk caught in the sun.

The rogue berry pearled out of my bark so real that when I wake, I taste the hard, round seed of it.

My father's eyesight is poor. He mistakes streetlamps for moons, asks me, What planet is this?

In a somewhere-else-dream maybe he misses her.

I almost tell him this, but I change my mind and we watch gods speared with electric fire burn down all the street.

Leah Saint Marie

Yellow Suit

I live in a suit of regret
aged yellow.

I wear it to work,
in the bathroom,
even to bed.

There's no button or zipper to release.
I finger the collar, stiff
as tweed left to dry.

I remember my body
slinging itself in the New River
among rainbow trout.

Sticking my head underwater
to the apocalypse of their hunger.

I once looked out the east window
at pines heavy with snow
before my suit,
when my youth and my love
were a sap pouring from me.

The Searcher

I've seen bees crawl to beauty—
some word coupled with immensity shouts
to them. They cannot help themselves.

They congregate to the sea like disarmed men
who saw love for the first time, and in the hollows
of their chest, they invented a new word.

You sit next to me,
my hair kicks in the Santa Ana—
and so I miss what you say before you move into water.

I see this—
the almost frailty of you
diving into it,
searching.

Spatial Recognition

This poem—like you—
is imperfect, and fears
how many times it will fail
before it ends.
It's afraid of the dark
that comes without thought
as it lies awake in bed
and stares at the small offense
of a loved one's back
turned toward it.

In the nothing between stanzas,
it wishes it were something—else,
something of use,
both wanting and not wanting
to be seen;
which is what you wish
as you brush your teeth on a Tuesday—
the promise of the day
like the palm of a hand retracting.

But then, what if a magician
turned all the mirrors off in
every room of every house
and this poem could only see itself
by looking at you—oh yes, you—
who once was a small body of intelligence before you could walk.
Would you find life
in the in-between spaces?
Would you then know
what you need to know?

The Man Who Sleeps

In dreams he swims as stars crash
against his anguish.

What is it the planets know
orbiting above the myth of his life?

Here is his answer. Here in this water
is his answer slipping past him.
He tries to grab it, but it roils all around him,
masterless.

He cannot know this upon waking,
unable—after a lifetime—
to translate the language of his dreams.

Farewell Ceremony

The bus waits, patient,
the destination doesn't matter.
A child cries, then laughs, then is silent
like its mother for the next year.

Because we are not holding hands
he returns the private's salute quickly.
It begins to rain.

His mother takes three photos of us.
I hold my hat somewhat awkwardly.
We'd fucked that morning
his fatigues around his ankles
like an ill-fitting noose—
a sad man's only suit,
the color of a dead animal's tongue.

I'm not in love—
he knows this.
There are parts to the ceremony I misstep
like a young girl's first dance—
the music incomprehensible.

A man yells, the soldiers thin out.
There is no time—
the bus has lost its indifference.
He leans in, rushed.
He tastes like me.
I'm embarrassed.
Suddenly my clothes don't fit.

I don't turn to look at him.
A small abuse.
It is nothing.
There isn't a sound
in my dreams for three days.
I have no comparison.

After the Rape

In Trastevere, Turkish jewelers haggle with me.
The silhouette of their legs through harem pants—
braids of muscle. Their chests roped
with gold chains. Their thick fingers rub together
as I pass them—sounds like paper
kissing paper. I buy nothing.

Miles of shops, bivouacs against yellow cracked walls.
Around the corner the Pantheon. The Vatican
past the Tiber. Each with its own dress code.
One asks of me for copper, the other for air.
I spare neither.

I take the train to Ostia Antica, where the river left the people.
Wisteria climbs the ruins. An empty pool. A trader's bar.
I put my ear to the stone of a bedroom window.
A dark seed rests on the sill. I place it in my mouth
and pray. I wait for it to speak to me.

Where there is no space for god, I grow my own.

Red Light

He yelled my name on N. 10th St.
The stoplight illuminated his eyes
red as a hunter's cap
buried in Birchwood
still
unmistakable.

I remember this in small details.
The scratch of his shoulders
beneath his shirt,
the high summer heat,
his drowned look
wet as a zoo animal
that questioned nothing.

His voice like buckshot said my name again.
It traveled like telephone wire straight to my ear.
I cannot pretend I didn't hear him.

There is an ache I know love by
when a man says my name.
A small strain—
the snap between syllables
the clip of his tongue around them
plunging.

I opened the car door—
a spiral eating itself,
at its center something inevitable.
I turned my high heel in the street—
it makes a sound like a fallen dove
stunned by the pavement
still flapping—
the taste of earth somehow obscene
in a mouth so used to atmosphere.

Leah Saint Marie

The Cage

For three decades the mirror
has told the same story:
I'm white. I'm female.

The men on the bus remind me
of these facts. Hating me.
Groping me. Lick their lips
and grab their crotch
like it's an exotic bird I want to see—
a rare bit of the jungle—
a fantastical beast that swallows
its own misery.

And because there's religion
and culture and rules,
I'm obligated to say thank you
and let them look inside
where I've hidden who I am
when I take off the skin
of my race and gender
and there's just the delicate song
of my bones.

Mornings

In the kitchen he drinks the last glass of milk—
it ribbons into him
and I pretend I know—
like the six songs the broken man sings—
his obscurity.

He smears his fingerprints over it—
even inside his throaty replies
there is silence
that wrecks me.

I lean closer
to this offering between us—
as he teaches me his language,
his tongue the last acrobat.

He removes his shirt,
shoes, face, erection for me,
to better see the oil that burns
where the heart destroys the calm phrases.

I leave the empty glass by the sink
so later when he's gone,
I can cup my ear to it
to hear the music say
what it must say.

Leah Saint Marie

Black Holes

Eventually the black holes will expand and contract and swallow all the space around them. Not even hungry. They'll do it anyway. The stars. The deer in the field. The paint in my bedroom. All eaten.

What will I miss more? Sunrise or sunset? Dogs or cats? Or, more tactile than that, kissing. The sound of the man I love sleeping next to me because he doesn't always sleep well. The scent of butter melting on the skillet when he makes dinner.

The black holes are coming. Inevitable. Not a single one of these moments survive. Not even this poem. I write it anyway. Compulsory. I do the dishes after dinner. He talks to me from the next room. What is it he says? I miss it. I walk in with soapy hands to hear it again. Somewhere, millions of miles away, it's beginning.

Salt

Even before we're born there's the taste of salt: the way our fathers sweat as they made us, the hard rim of the cervix, the horned shell of our body collapsing.

Then later, the sharp taste of ocean as we kiss—a palace of spice— the trade route to ecstasy.

Then later still, it's the private flavor of our grief when our kingness caves. We know what the widow knows, we share the same pillow.

It rings our body citadel—here in this oneness, millions—even in fire the fine grains drop from us as rubies.

Galaxies

There's a planet full of lost things. On it is everyone's virginity, next door to lost minds, which is catty-cornered to a generation. My St. Christopher necklace is surely there; the one from Poland circa 1942, small as the pad of a child's pinky, the ones that when severed can still grow back— the pied flesh, like the scarred arm of a starfish.

These things are lost even from each other, so inside this planet is a smaller planet of loneliness. Here, nothing weighs anything—that's sorrow's job.

Somehow, we find them. Both planets. Inevitable in that inky infinity that we itch to understand, where we all visit—

we wayward astronauts,
we small gods of science,
we haunted animals.

Five Blackbirds

I walk in the shadow of five blackbirds
dark and secret as the boxes men keep
full of the ache that made them.
I pull an orange from a tree
that the neighbor says won't be ripe
until January. Inside, the fruit is bitter.

There once was the care of someone else washing me,
who kept soap from my eyes.
This too is a box—a mouth
where bitterness turns into song
when the hands let go.

There is a fear in living that the unborn—
building an obelisk many miles above them—
cannot tempt God to let them know.

These five shadows follow me
like names I gave to my unborn children.
Each a perfect syllable.
I cannot wash my hands from knowing.

I count the days till a year from now
I will be awake in bed with the open window and the snow
and a long-held dream will leave me.

About the Author

Leah Saint Marie is an investigative journalist turned filmmaker. During her time as a reporter for the Innocence Institute, she helped exonerate a man from prison who had spent 25 years wrongfully convicted. As a filmmaker, she wrote the award-winning documentary, *Price of Honor,* which got Yaser Said on the FBI's Top Ten Most Wanted (the documentary led to his eventual arrest in 2021). Her script, *Spoonful of Sugar,* premiered at Fantastic Fest (2022) and sold to Shudder (where it can now be streamed). Her short film, *Good Girl,* won the Paris International Film Festival. For two years she served as a field producer for the social justice documentary film company, Brave New Films, where she traveled around the United States on a Ford grant interviewing youth activists. She's the producer of the podcasts, Before the Fade, and Pitch! the latter of which she co-hosts. As of this publication, she lives and writes in Los Angeles, CA, along with her cat, Edith Piaf.

Acknowledgments

To the ones who weathered the storm with me: Friends, Muses, Teachers. Hailee, Sean, Nathan, John, Missie, Anne W/S, Zac, & Alyssa L.

And with much gratitude to journals in which some of these pieces have appeared:

"Salt," "The Garden," "The Elk," "Galaxies" in *Terrain.*
"Seed" in *Conduit*.
"Farmboy" in *ARC Magazine*.
"Block Island Trip," "Ursa Minor," "Nine Minutes,"
"The Architect" in *LitBreak.*

"Trinitia Church" in *Rutgers University Press.*